~ Inside your skin ~

Jan Folkert

Inside your skin

25 poems

For beautiful people

ISBN 978-90-817103-4-3

NUR 306

© 2014
Jan F. Bouman (publisher)
jan.bouman@xs4all.nl

1st edition

This publications is protected by copyright and permission must be obtained from the publisher prior to any prohibited reproduction, storage in a retrieval system, or transmission in any form or by any means, electronic, mechanical, photocopying, recording or likewise.

Contents

Inside your skin

Jan Folkert

- ..1.. Once my darling
- ..2.. Flow of winds
- ..3.. Morrow
- ..4.. War bride
- ..5.. Different
- ..6.. Leave him
- ..7.. Like still water
- ..8.. Muse
- ..9.. Lure
- ..10.. Shadow
- ..11.. Oil of Nard
- ..12.. Even they?
- ..13.. Mary's troubles
- ..14.. Seduced, betrayed, caught
- ..15.. Colors
- ..16.. September
- ..17.. Mother of Mused
- ..18.. Dead you are my love
- ..19.. Senseless silhouette
- ..20.. Dew dream
- ..21.. Water ripples
- ..22.. My mother
- ..23.. Quiet together
- ..24.. Camber
- ..25.. Ireland

Once my darling

Once my darling, we were one.
We shared our secrets,
unspoken - with each other.

>Where to, my dear, are you going?
>Where is that other world
>I cannot reach?

Sometimes your hand reaches to me
and you caress my memory,
as volatile as the morning mist.

And then, when the sun rises again,
tears evaporate with the dew,
I wander off with you ... and I ask:

>Stay a while. Show your eyes.
>Gray traces of time.
>Mirrors of my melancholy, silent.

Hoping that this day I can live
with your other world.

Flow of winds

gently floats your last breath
escaping loneliness
of your heart, weary
finally fully free
away from pain
to where you are nothing
and nothing is in all

together with old souls
your breath joins willingly
the flow of winds,
that goes on for ages
as a song of sighs

and the smallest gust
   (falling of a leaf)
   (moving a flower)
   (wings of a bee)
belongs to you

and then you really
give meaning and purpose
to faltering life

Morrow

Night pulls away from black above
with wavering glow, watery in the sky
far cry, bestial and covered with hoarfrost
that smells round when movements are visible
whip of light strikes our feet
lashes widen and extinguish, becoming day.

War bride   .. 4 ..

taking you
off the battlefield

how we accidentally
touched each other
in a daze
of despair
and diffidence
of debt

because we
and not the other
are here today

to live
to remember
to keep silent
and to make love

when we finally die
war is covered

Different .. 5 ..

it's not you who is lost, it's the world inside you

I call out to your eyes while you almost drown
in dancing scents, red, yellow and blue

light of day you keep in your pockets
as toppings for the night

when I come
yes, if I come

Leave him　　　　　　　　　　　　　　　　　.. 6 ..

he is happy
joking and laughing
in his own constellation

the voices in his head
pity us because of our silence
but we have no choice

Like still water

Like still water
- seemingly undisturbed
by the storm
that rages around us -
you keep playing.

But if undercurrent
meets the light of day,
water wrinkles
and you ask, so seriously
where I live...

I take your little hand
And silent words flow
in the drift of our bond.

Muse   .. 8 ..

Lips moved through vapored wisps of your herbal tea.
After two times they shifted into laugh, shaped with light voice
in visual sounds. Words I saw, felt and wanted to capture.
You spoke them - only with your eyes, sometimes –
and it was as it is, without intent.
No will or expectation broke the spell.
Only that thrill of delight and stimulation
that flowed with the words. A well, one with your voice,
your eyes, your skin and the sensual curves of your body.

You are beautiful, my Muse
as only a Muse can be.

Lure

After days of depression
the wind turns in my back.

the lure
of a new lover.

In a vortex of euphoria
I reach for happiness.

Shadow   .. 10 ..

Shadow of disgust follows me.
Small and naked I had no choice.
Smothered in dark light. His power.
Thirty years - more - he stays with me.
A haze, a shadow. Always present.

And for him?
Only a wandering star I am.
Forgotten in his trace of molest.

Oil of Nard .. 11 ..

~inspired by the Songs of Salomon ~

On the mountains I searched for herbs to make your balm. High.
Looking down at my shadow through your eyes, through your hands.
By your ascetic body of a man, a beautiful man
Let me anoint you. Not your head like a king,
not your lips like a lover, but your feet. Because I am ...
I'm a woman. A woman with dreams from a deep well.
Attraction of your mind and resistance of your skin. My hand,
the oil. Storms in my body, my belly, my breasts.

Vortex of confusion by your voice, your word.
Without reason without form.
Flowing balm of Nard.
Heaven, as soil at your feet.

Even they? .. 12 ..

where was your power
that night, when you
were led away
to egypt?

did you play with them
while you could not save them
were you too human?

was there no one
who cursed you
after you, however small,
fled the bloody sword of herod

hanna, suzanna and salome,
how did you later
comfort those mothers?

did they follow you?
even they?
and did they ever
close your words in their hearts?

Mary's troubles

Gifted?
Blessed among women?

Is that it? If I, provoked by his delusion,
find him at the square, sitting with old men?

Was it the angel who mentioned that shadow
of blessing? That backside of grace.

Is it madness? His growth, half-grown,
together with blindness for my love.

His surprise! Is it pride?
His Father, yes always his great Father.

How long am I allowed to be his mother?
When he will disown me too, and his brothers?

Ordeal beyond fulfillment.
Which fulfillment?

When will he blend into the Father, his great Father,
and deliver us from his manhood?

Or from his godhood?

Seduced, betrayed, caught .. 14 ..

Seduced, betrayed, caught.
Dragged from the arms of my lover.
Stupid, stupid, stupid I am to trust him.
He would protect me.
Rescue me from the hands of my enemies.
Where is he?
Is he pleading for me?
Taking the blame,
any blame whatsoever?
Nothing!
No shadow of his love.
I see his dim shape
on his way home, to his wife, his honor.
His reputation, worth more than my life.
The stones on my soul hurt more
than those on my body.
Thrown by rough men of the law.
Blameless they can rape me.
Loyal, as they say, to my infidelity.

But then there's that One,
a Teacher at the temple.
He reaches deeper than the others
even than my lover ever did.
Who writes in the sand
and makes it whole in a silent moment. All of it.
Away from men, stones and blame.

Until we are alone together, the two of us,
because no first stone was thrown.

Colors

I do not know
if the rose can see its red
and the dolphin
his own gray

because the light in my eye
colors in the shade
of my existence
and through your eyes
I can only dream

I don't know
if my blue
also fills your sky

when we are together

September

red shines low
and leaves its print
on space still full, between branches
reaching for birds that swarm
against the tilt
of the earth

and the source rotates slowly
in the mists of cobwebs,
giving its shining to us

Mother of Muses

The weeks
after I gave you to the earth,
- In your home, chair, bed -
you lived in a thousand shades
one by one through my hands
and died again,
as the teapot,
still resonating our long talks,
fell into shards.

Your life, evoked
from clippings, rugs,
postcards and other trifles
like hairs in the curlers
I found and I stroked.
Touch that was left to me.

But the image of your smile stays
with me, with so many. Mother ...

of all muses.

Dead you are my love

dead you are my love

the day sounds
like box of wood and
rough and dull and void
of you

but still, and then
the space is filled
with sound
a tone
that scrapes, that shapes
that draws roses as circles
around my heart that beats

dead you are
my love I live

Senseless silhouette .. 19 ..

deep, deep,
when you were drawn
lifeless through my breath
and my cry could not wake you
when I, in despair
too soon
contracted my body
I wanted to go with you,
away from pale blood
on your little hands
and on your still eyes,
along with your beautiful,
senseless silhouette

then your voice laughed
not in front of me, where you lay
but inside of me, behind me
and as a painful bliss
you stay with me
always

Dew dream

come

dream with me the dew
down from the clouds
where our eyes
at the first flash
liberate the sun

then comes brilliance
filling mist with feeling
making world pregnant
with floating light

environed by white
that carry birds
whose wings
press down pearl drops
on the grass below

and in the blue veins
of our bodies

until the red glow settles
and slumber disappears

Water ripples

water ripples
stone breaks the surface
opens your skin
vibration after caress

as quickly as it opens
it closes again

unanswered
where the stone
where the caress
is kept

My mother

My mother was the cadence
of her own song of words
whose verses secretly burnt
when she was claimed
by the rhythm of her time.

My mother was 'thoughts'
in tranquil sounding cups
on the counter
and in solidified grief
sliced as memories
that served as duty.

My mother is conscience
of my heart's deepest cavities
that in reluctant light
opens up recognition
that together, we are
two. Two of a kind.

Quiet together

both busy
clock ticks
paper rustles
as if it burns
softly crackles
in the fire
of each other's warmth
where your space
meets mine

filling stillness
together

Camber

Seven months of camber
you carry.
Framed with adornment
of deep black hair
and eyes as beacons
at the south coast
of the Black Sea.

Fortunate the child
that takes shelter in you
and soon finds a muse
of beauty and style
as mother.

Ireland

When twilight falls
on the green shades,
stones slowly tend to
the whisper of night.
Old souls will come
from ruins to life
and cry, and sing
of love and hunger.

Trembling,
slowly merging
in rhythm and rhyme.
Songs that tell
of homecoming, out of the
hollows between the stones
on green blankets
that cover up the dead.

They pull up, narrowly
along the living, beating hearts
and silently share emotions
of origin, attached
to their old volatile bodies
dissolute, mobile
as shadows falling on rain.

As the sea crashes
on the Cliffs of Moher
wisps of mist come.
Souls return from the new land.
Everywhere, among the tombs
and ruined churches,
the wind sighs and cries
of encounter and reunion.

But as the sun rises
over the eastern hills,
sighs seek their hideouts
and the old land forces me
to nostalgia
for the green slopes
and petrified moss
on a Celtic cross.

www.ingramcontent.com/pod-product-compliance
Lightning Source LLC
LaVergne TN
LVHW011431080426
835512LV00005B/387